HOW TO PRAY FOR

YOUR LOVED ONES

By Kathy Casto

ISBN 978-1-879545-02-1 REVISED EDITION

Dedication

To my husband and two children - it was through their struggles that I became strong. It was because of their struggles that I ran to the Lord for help, and He taught me HOW TO PRAY for my loved ones.

Contents

Preface

There are many excellent books one can read and study on the subject of prayer (see Preferred Reading List on page); however, you will never learn to pray until you actually begin praying. This book is intended only as a "tool" to help you in the place of prayer. Through this material you will learn not only the importance of praying the Word over the problems you face daily, but also "how to pray" the Word over your husband, wife, children, lost loved ones, pastor, and nation.

You do not have to struggle in a continual stream of financial reverses, physical ailments, and family explosions. You can rise up in the mighty name of Jesus and scatter the forces of the enemy that have targeted your life for destruction:

"Give us aid against the enemy, for *the help of man is worthless. With God* we will gain the victory and *He* will trample down our enemies." (Psalm 60:11, 12 NIV) [emphasis mine]

"You are my King, O God; *command victories* for Jacob (us). *Through you* we push back our enemies; *through your name* we trample our foes." (Psalm 44:4, 5) [Emphasis mine]

My prayer for you who study this material is that you will receive the desires of your heart for your loved ones. Your family will become like the holy men of old *"whose weakness was turned to strength; and who became powerful in battle and routed foreign armies."* (Hebrews 11:34 NIV)

May your ears be sensitized to the voice of the Holy Spirit as you set your course to follow Him in prayer; and may you turn many from the snares of death as you drink deeply from the "fountain of life" found in the teachings of the wise. (Proverbs 13:14 NIV)

The Calm Before the Storm

The House that Kathy Built

For many years, I led a relatively problem-free life with little more to deal with than a very small budget, an occasional disagreement with my husband, and a few bruises on my toddler's knees. After the first few years of adjusting to each other and the demands of ministry (or should I say learning to submit to my husband), our marriage was strong and we enjoyed working together.

I thought I was being the wise woman of Proverbs 14:1 who *"builds her house."* After all, I wasn't arguing with him anymore or criticizing him in everything he tried to do as I had done the first five years we were married. On the contrary, I had learned to play the piano, attended every activity, meeting, counsel, retreat or advance on the calendar, as well as opened our home for dinners, prayer meetings, music rehearsals, and guest speakers. I smiled, always sat on the front row, and was good at keeping my mouth shut. *"Even a fool is thought wise if he keeps silent and discerning if he holds his tongue."* (Proverbs 17:28 NIV)

It worked beautifully for a while. Everyone thought I was the perfect pastor's wife; everyone, that is, except me. Deep inside I knew the Lord wanted something else from me besides my best efforts, or even my talents and abilities. The Lord wanted me. He wanted a close, intimate relationship that I had never taken the "time" to develop. He wanted me walking beside my husband spiritually. I always had the mental picture of John and myself going through life with him floating about ten feet above my head while I walked on the earth. I kept thinking that if we were both "heavenly minded," would we be any "earthly" good? Who do you think was inspiring this line of thought?

> Psalm 127:1 (NIV) says, "Unless the Lord builds the house, its builders labor in vain. Unless the Lord watches over the city, the watchmen stand guard in vain."

Although I was building to the best of my ability, I was building in my own strength. I was not allowing the Lord to build through me. I did not realize how dangerous this was to our family and ministry or how ignorant I was to the strategies the enemy was weaving against us until the attack was launched. Satan systematically hit every member of our little family and every area of our lives - physically, spiritually, and financially.

Remember the expression, "when it rains, it pours"? I always heard this in the context of many troubles pouring into one's life at one time. This is a perfect example of what is happening in the spirit realm when Satan targets you and your family. He is *like a roaring lion looking for someone to devour* (I Peter 5:8 NIV). He will destroy your health, your finances, your family, marriage, and your very life, if possible. Do not be deceived or caught off guard by the "calm before the storm."

In the Midst of the Storm

The Winds of Change Began to Blow

The storms began to blow into our lives the year our second little girl was born. My husband became extremely frustrated in the ministry, disappointed with our particular denomination, and discouraged with certain physical problems. The year our four year old started kindergarten, our baby began to develop one ear infection after another which caused hours of pain for her and sleepless nights for everyone else. There were no medical cures for our physical problems, only vague theories and fleeting hopes. It seemed the closer we drew to the Lord, the worse our situations became.

It was during these desperate days that I began to hear in my spirit, "If you don't pray for your husband, who will?" "If you don't pray for your children, who will?" The next question did not seem unusual, living at that time just outside of Washington, D.C.: "If you don't pray for your nation, its lawyers, judges and leaders, who will?"

The Lord was allowing the cloak of maturity and responsibility to fall upon my shoulders. I began to realize that we are responsible for our generation and for the time and place we have been given to live out our days upon the earth.

"...You are my God. My times are in your hands..." (Psalm 31:14 [b], 15 [a] NIV)

"...and he determined the times set for them and the *exact places where they should live.*

God did this so that men would seek him and perhaps reach out for him and find him, though he is not far from each one of us." (Acts 17:26 [b] and 27 NIV)

As I prayed for my family and asked the Lord to build through me, I realized that I did not have the proper "tools" to build a strong house. All the activities and ministries in which I had been involved for many years had not prepared me spiritually for the storms blowing into our lives. I did not understand at this point that the storms were caused by the powers of darkness determined to destroy us, and I certainly didn't know how to fight in the spirit realm.

Powers of darkness! You mean financial reverses, sickness, job promotions or losses, and family problems could be influenced by the spirit realm? Read the words of Paul and judge for yourself:

"Finally, be strong in the Lord and in his mighty power. Put on the armor of God so that *you can take your stand against the devil's schemes.* For our struggle is not against flesh and blood, but against the rulers, against the authorities, against the powers of this dark world and against the spiritual forces of evil in the heavenly realms." (Ephesians 6:10-12 NIV) [Emphasis mine]

The Tools to Build His House

As I continued to answer the promptings of the Spirit to seek the Lord daily in behalf of my family, I became very frustrated. I knew the Lord was asking me to spend an hour in prayer with Him, but after fifteen minutes, I was lost. I would make myself stay there an hour, but I felt like I was wandering aimlessly during my prayer time with no sense of direction and certainly no "tools" in hand.

The Lord heard my heart's cry, however, and began to send the answers to me just as it says in Jeremiah 33:3 (NIV):

"Call to me and I will answer you and tell you great and unsearchable things you do not know."

Interestingly enough soon after that prayer for help, I received a copy of Dr. Larry Lea's prayer teaching in the mail and knew I had received "manna from heaven." After listening to this pattern based on Matthew 6, I had no difficulty spending an hour in prayer as I followed the outline. However, I began to feel odd because I went to bed early in order to get up early to pray. I did not know anyone else who did such a thing.

God's hand was orchestrating the events around our lives and brought the world leader of prayer at that time to our area --Dr. Paul Yonggi Cho, pastor of the great 800,000+-member church in Seoul, Korea. He made a statement that changed my life. Dr. Cho said, "The American culture is not geared for early morning prayer. In order to become established in prayer, you will have to change your lifestyle. Your day will have to begin and end earlier." That was all I needed to pursue the course I had chosen to find the answers to our problems.

The **first tool**, then, is daily, consistent prayer through a systematic outline — preferably the Lord's Prayer.

The **second tool**, I soon discovered, was the Word of God. Not just a daily reading of a couple of chapters to fulfill our Christian duty, but intimate, quality time in the Word. A time when you ask the Lord to *"open your eyes that you may see wonderful things in His law"* (Psalm 119:18 NIV) and to *"give you understanding of His commands"* (Psalm 119:73).

Dr. Cho says "something supernatural" takes place when you pray an hour. Dr. Larry Lea says "something special" happens when you pray an hour daily and take time to study His Word. I have found that your ears become sensitized to the voice of your Shepherd. You "hear" His voice as your read each day. You "hear" His voice in the voice of your pastor or teachers. You "hear" the heart's cry behind the spoken words of your children or husband. You will also recognize a voice that is contrary to the Word instantly:

> "My sheep hear my voice, and I know them, and they follow me." (John 10:27)

> "...he (the Shepherd) goes ahead of them, and his sheep follow him because they know his voice. But they will never follow a stranger; in fact, they will run away from him because they do not recognize a stranger's voice." (John 10:4, 5 NIV)

Your eyes will begin to see life through the eyes of the Spirit rather than the disillusioned fantasy world of the moviemakers or the unfortunate scars from physical or emotional abuse, broken relationships and shattered dreams. You will begin to understand how our Father deals with man, that He works everything together in your behalf, and that He changes what has been intended for evil in your life by the enemy into something good.

Your mouth will become a fountain of life for the Word is flowing into you every morning or evening as you "feed" in His green pastures (Proverbs 10:11). You will speak life instead of death; your tongue will be as choice silver (Proverbs 10:20); and your lips will nourish many (Proverbs 10:21).

I would like to encourage you to start reading one Proverb and five Psalms each days for wisdom and encouragement. After you have become accustomed to this schedule and begin to desire more of the Word, you can begin a systematic approach to read the Bible through periodically. I enjoy the Psalms and Proverbs each morning in addition to five chapters from the Old Testament and three from the New Testament. This allows me to read the Bible through three times annually.

The following reading schedule will help you determine how much to read daily in order to accomplish your goals for the year. In addition to the daily reading in Proverbs and Psalms, add:

3 chapters for annual completion;

5 1/2 chapters for semi-annual completion;

8 chapters for completion every four months;

11 chapters for quarterly completion;

16 chapters for completion every 2 months;

33 chapters for monthly completion.

As you begin to saturate your being with the Word, the Spirit will prompt you to pray specific scriptures over your problems.

This brings us to our **third tool**, a prayer notebook. This book is in actuality your "Beginner's Prayer Notebook." Just as a musician starts on the beginner level or a child learns to read with kindergarten materials, this book is a beginning point.

You will see many prayers answered as you pray the scriptures compiled under the different headings; however, as you become skilled in using the Word and "hearing" what the Spirit is saying to you concerning your family, you will begin to use your own scriptures for different circumstances that will arise in your life. You will not be facing the same problems next year for you will learn to overcome through the blood of the Lamb and the word of your testimony (Revelation 12:11). Your prayer life and prayer notebook will grow and expand as you drive the enemy out of the different areas of your life and learn to possess the land the Lord has given you as an inheritance.

The Weapons of our Warfare

We have been examining the tools to build a strong house:

(1) Consistent daily prayer following a systematic pattern;

(2) The Word of God;

(3) A prayer notebook.

Have you noticed how quickly the tools to build a strong house convert into "weapons of warfare" as we become skilled workmen? I am reminded of the passage in Joel 4 where the warriors beat their plowshares into swords and their pruning hooks into spears. In times of war, we must pick up our swords for battle: *"Let the weakling say, "I am strong!"* (Joel 3:10 NIV). Read the words of David:

"Do you see a man skilled in his work? He will serve before Kings and not obscure men." (Proverbs 22:29 NIV)

Faithfulness in the little things (your first responsibilities in the home or on the job) prepares you to rule over many things (Matthew 25:21) including the powers of darkness (Luke 10:19). You will become a mighty warrior in the Lord's army. David's victories over the lion and the bear prepared him for the great battle with Goliath, which brought him into the King's service, the King's family, and eventually the King's throne.

Vision of a Warrior

When I first began to pray through the Lord's Prayer and put on the armor each day, I saw a vision of a female warrior. I knew the Lord was showing me a picture of my spiritual state. The only problem with the warrior was that she was reclining on a chaise asleep! I was not aware that a battle was raging around me. As I began to recognize the source of my problems over the next few months, I saw the warrior sit up, and within a few more months, stand. I was not yet ready for battle, however, for my sword and shield were hanging loosely at my sides.

After our family moved to Rockwall, an Elder's wife at Church on the Rock encouraged us to pray the Word of God over our husbands. She said, "You can always pray the will of God if you pray the Word of God." When I heard those words, a light of understanding flooded into my spirit. My whole prayer life began to change. Not wanting to limit this to just my husband, I began to pray the Word over my children, my family, our finances, everything! If the

Word of God was the will of God for our lives, I no longer had to struggle in doubt and confusion concerning God's will.

When I began to weave the Word throughout the Lord's Prayer, I began to see all the strongholds the enemy had held so long in our lives come down. Our weapons are mighty to the pulling down of strongholds. (II Corinthians 10:4)

Within a few months our youngest daughter's severe allergies subsided; and my husband changed before my eyes into a strong, powerful man of prayer determined to fulfill God's purpose in his life.

Can you imagine what the warrior looked like the next time I saw her? She had a warrior's stance, feet slightly apart, knees bent, and ready to spring into action. The sword and the shield were held in position, and interestingly, there were little dark circles all around her feet. When I asked the Lord what these were, He reminded me of all the battles I had been fighting for my family in prayer. Each flaming arrow had been hurled at us with a specific target in the enemy's sight: my baby's health, my husband's calling, and even our marriage. However, for every fiery assault, the shield had quenched the flames and the sword had cast the devourer under my feet! Hallelujah!

The Sword of the Spirit

I would like to share with you the scriptures the Lord brought to my attention to confirm the use of the Word in my prayer life.

In the fourth chapter of Matthew, we find that *"Jesus was led by the Spirit into the desert to be tempted by the devil"* (Matthew 4:1). This was immediately after his baptism by John with the descent of the Spirit upon him in the form of a dove and just prior to the launch of His public ministry. It was during this time of transition that the enemy tempted Jesus. Let us take a close look at Jesus' responses to the enemy. In every case, Jesus quoted the **Word.** There were no arguments, discussions, or debates – only the simple, pure Word of God.

Jesus answered, **"It is written**: 'Man does not live on bread alone, but on every **word** that comes from the mouth of God.'" (Matthew 4:4 NIV) [Emphasis mine]

Jesus answered him, **"It is also written**: 'Do not put the Lord your God to the test.'" (Matthew 4:7 NIV) [Emphasis mine]

Jesus said to him, "Away from me, Satan! **For it is written**: 'Worship the Lord your God, and serve him only.'" (Matthew 4:10 NIV) [Emphasis mine]

In the book of Revelation, we find that Jesus will use this same strategy against Satan when He returns:

"...out of his mouth came a sharp double-edged sword." (Revelation 1:16 NIV)

"...I will soon come to you and will fight against them with the sword of my mouth." (Revelation 2:16 NIV)

"Out of his mouth comes a sharp sword with which to strike down the nations." (Revelation 19:15 NIV)

If the Word was the response of Jesus to the temptations of the enemy in the desert and will be His strategy when He returns, shouldn't we learn from His example and pick up the sword to fight?

Let us examine the armor in Ephesians 6 for a moment. The only offensive weapon in the armor is "the sword of the Spirit, which is the word of God." The remainder of the armor is defensive. Of course, all the pieces of the armor are important: you cannot go into battle without your protective covering. However, if you never use your sword against the enemy, he will never be defeated. He will assault you, your loved ones, your finances, and every area of your life until you finally give up, blame God, and turn from Him. Satan is the master deceiver!

On the other hand, the moment you pick up your sword to fight, the enemy trembles. He cannot stand against the Word. Read the following promises:

"So is my word that goes out from my mouth: It will not return to me empty, but will accomplish what I desire and achieve the purpose for which I sent it." (Isiah 55:11 NIV)

"He sends his commands to the earth; his word runs swiftly." (Psalm 147:15 NIV)

"They overcame him by the blood of the Lamb and by the word of their testimony." (Revelation 12:11 NIV)

"Your word, O Lord, is eternal, it stands firm in the heavens." (PSALM 119:18 NIV)

"Praise the Lord, you his angels, you mighty ones who do his bidding, who obey his word." (PSALM 103:20 NIV)

The Word of God is the will of God for your life. It is not God's will for you to be sick, depressed, discouraged, financially ruined, or distraught over your family! Let the promise found in I John 5:14 (NIV) sink into your spirit:

"This is the assurance we have in approaching God: that if we ask anything according to his will, he hears us. And if we know that he hears us – whatever we ask – we know that we have what we asked of him."

Whatever problem you face, the Lord has the answer in His Word for you. My pastor, Dr. Larry Lea (author of *Could You Not Tarry One Hour?*), said, "Focus on the promise, not the problem." The way the Lord has taught me to do this is to pray a specific scripture or scriptures over each problem we face in our family, church, nation, or on the mission fields.

I have included many of the scriptures I use over different situations in the latter portion of this book. In fact, these particular scriptures are the reason for this book. I wanted to share what I have learned in the place of prayer in order that you who read this and implement it into your prayer life would grow strong as you learn to use the Word as a sword against the enemy. Please allow me to give you a brief example of using the Word in your prayer life.

The Sharpening of the Sword

(Scriptures for Husbands)

As a wife, you know and love your husband better than anyone else; therefore, the Lord will show you the weak areas in his life that He will not entrust to others. He does not do this for you to point out publicly, expose to your friends and relatives, or nag him daily to correct him. No, the Lord wants you to pray for him. He will give you a specific scripture to counteract this weak point so that your husband may grow strong in the Lord through your life-giving prayers.

When I sense a particular need in my husband's life, I pray Proverbs 21:1 (NIV) over him:

"The king's heart is in the hand of the Lord; he directs it like a watercourse wherever he pleases."

With this scripture I am acknowledging that John is my spiritual authority and that Jesus is his head (Ephesians 5:23). It is the Lord's responsibility to change or correct him, not mine. I am only coming into agreement in prayer with what I feel the Holy Spirit wants to do in his life (not my selfish desires). Next, I pray the scripture that addresses the need.

If the need concerns his relationship with our children, I pray Malachi 4:6 (NIV):

"...turn the hearts of the fathers to their children (*Father, turn John's heart to our children*) and the hearts of the children to their fathers" *(and let the hearts of my children be drawn to John).*

If he becomes frustrated with the work at the office, I pray Psalm 90:12 or Exodus 17:12 (NIV):

"Teach us *(him)* to number our *(his)* days aright, that we *(he)* may gain a heart of wisdom. (Psalm 90:12)

"Aaron and Hur held his *(Moses)* hands up - one on one side, one on the other - so that his hands remained steady till sunset." (Exodus 17:12 NIV) *(Father, send John an Aaron and Hur to hold his hands steady and stand beside him as he labors for you).*

If there is a financial matter that needs my husband's attention, I pray Matthew 25:21:

"...thou has been faithful over a few things, I will make thee ruler over many things." (Matthew 25:21 [b] NIV)

"Lord, help my husband to be found faithful in the few things in our lives that you can entrust us with greater things; let us be found faithful in handling worldly wealth in order that we may receive true riches."

I do not nag him about these things when he comes home or even offer advice *unless HE asks me.* I have found time and time again that the Holy Spirit starts working immediately in his heart. Within two or three days he will come home and say, "We have got to spend more time with the kids. I have been a bear lately," or "We have got to look into that insurance. I can't think of anything else; it has been on my mind all day," or "You know, God has been telling me what to do in the morning during prayer, and I am getting so much done at the office now."

The Lord dropped all these things into his heart and he thought it was his idea! These are very simple illustrations of using the Word in your everyday lives; but as you see the answers to the smaller problems in life, you will grow stronger for the larger battles.

Through your prayer and encouraging words, you will become the wise woman who is building her house rather than tearing it down with her own hands (Proverbs 14:1). You will be the wife of noble character who brings her husband *"good, not harm, all the days of her life"* (Proverbs31:12); and who *"speaks with wisdom, and faithful instruction is on her tongue"* (Proverbs 31:26).

The Word of God is truth, and what it says about your husband is God's will for his life. Do not be deceived by the circumstances you face today. They are only a smoke screen to discourage you and keep you from praying. Do not speak negative words over your situation. This only distorts your vision and keeps your eyes focused on the problem instead of the promise and on what "appears to be" rather than truth, which is the Word of God.

The following scriptures show us the importance of words and their effect upon others:

"The tongue has the power of life and death..." (Proverbs 18:21 [a] NIV)

"Reckless words pierce like a sword, but the tongue of the wise brings healing." (Proverbs 12:18 NIV)

"The mouth of the righteous is a fountain of life..." (Proverbs 10:11 [a] NIV)

"The lips of the righteous nourish many..." (Proverbs 10:21 [a] NIV)

When you pray the Word, it will build your faith for *"faith cometh by hearing, and hearing by the word of God."* (Romans 10:17) You pray the Word, you hear the Word: your faith increases. Morning by morning your faith grows stronger until you no longer see the situation as it appears momentarily, but you see it through the eyes of the Spirit, confident that God is working in your behalf. It is only a matter of time before you receive the answer.

I like what Dr. B. J. Willhite, founder of National Call to Prayer, says: "If you have enough faith to pray, you have enough faith to move the hand of God." His example is the account of Peter's release from prison because the church decided to pray. However, when Peter arrived at the prayer meeting, they did not believe it was him. They only had enough faith to pray, but the Lord heard their cries and delivered Peter.

"The righteous cry out, and the Lord hears them; he delivers them from all their troubles." (Psalm 34:17 NIV)

I always ask the Lord to show my husband to me through the eyes of the Spirit. I want to see him as God sees him and know what God wants to do through him.

"Open my ears, Lord, to hear what your spirit is saying to me concerning him." This allows me to pray what our Father desires for him.

As we show ourselves faithful in the small areas of our lives and families, the Lord will entrust us with greater responsibilities, if we are willing. He will begin to use us to pray for our pastors, friends, employers or employees, national leaders, and others. All He wants are those who will make themselves available to be led by the Spirit during their time of prayer.

Freedom

I would like to release you from any form of bondage with which the enemy would try to entrap you. Do not feel pressured to pray every scripture over everyone every day. There have been days, weeks, or even months when the Spirit has had me praying the same scriptures over a particular circumstance. It is during these times that you are birthing something the Lord wants to accomplish in the spirit realm.

You will have days, though, when you go to prayer and you feel burdened just for your pastor, or just for your husband or children. It is all right to pray your burden that day instead of your notebook full of scriptures the Lord has been pouring into you. The heaviness you feel in your heart is from the Lord. You are being given a "special assignment," if you will. There is an emergency in the heavenlies that needs your prayer support that morning.

When you choose to pray His burden for the day, you can rest assured that He will take care of your family and circumstances. *"Delight yourself in the Lord and he will give you the desires of your heart."* (Psalm 37:4 NIV)

I was agreeing in prayer with a friend for an adoption and her husband's recommitment in his walk with the Lord. Yet every time she came to prayer, all she could pray for was my husband, the pastor in charge of the prayer meeting. She did not understand this and even asked me about it. Although she had many needs to pray over, she was faithful to pray the burden laid on her heart daily. The Lord was working all things together for her good (Romans 8:28). He was using her intercessory prayer gift to strengthen my husband as He took her focus off the seemingly unanswered prayers for her baby and husband. The Lord had already answered her prayers; the answer was just not evident yet.

"Before they call I will answer; while they are still speaking I will hear." (Isaiah 65:24)

Within a couple of months, my friend received her baby boy and her husband began to attend church regularly.

Please do not grow discouraged if your prayers are not answered the first day. Some prayers are answered immediately, some take a few days, but others take months or even years. The key is to never give up. On the contrary, we must stay alert to recognize our answers when the Lord brings them into our lives.

Because we know God is working all things together for good for those that love Him and are the called according to His purpose (Romans 8:28), we must realize that the answer to *one* of our prayers may affect five or six individuals or families: a job promotion, marriage restorations, a new baby or adoption. He hears your prayers the *first* day you pray and begins to work good for all concerned. That is why we experience *a time delay* in the Lord answering our prayers in the heavenlies and seeing the results physically on earth.

A prayer journal will help you record the answers to your prayers, the time element involved and perhaps even the people affected. Your faith will be greatly increased as you periodically review the Lord's hand moving in your life.

Marilyn Hickey once said prayers were like seeds that are watered daily. Different ones take different lengths of time to sprout and grow. Whenever I become discouraged, I ask the Lord to open my eyes that I can see His blessings when they come (Read Jeremiah chapter 17 concerning the man who depends upon flesh for strength and does not see the Lord's blessings when they come as opposed to the man who trusts in the Lord).

John Wesley said, "God does nothing but in answer to prayer."

Dick Eastman says, "When you pray, something will take place in the heavenlies that would not have happened without your prayers."

Dr. B. J. Willhite says, "If you have enough faith to pray, you have enough faith to move the hand of God."

Dr. Larry Lea says, "It may not be easy, but it will be worth it."

I would like to encourage you to use the Matthew 6 outline with the scriptures interwoven through it on a daily basis. This is your offensive weapon, your plan to win. The Lord will use you to win great victories for Him and may even assign you to a special task force occasionally (those days when He gives you a special burden).

Let us look at Psalm 44:6-8 as we prepare ourselves for battle:

"I do not trust in my bow, my sword does not bring me victory; but you put our adversaries to shame. In God we make our boast all day long and we will praise your name forever."

How to Pray for Yourself

The following scriptures have been included to help you, as you pray, invite the Holy Spirit to take control of your life daily and to keep you sensitive to His voice:

"THY KINGDOM COME, THY WILL BE DONE IN MY LIFE AS IT IS IN HEAVEN.

Father, I present myself to you today as a living sacrifice, holy and acceptable unto you which is my reasonable service. I will not conform any longer to the pattern of this world, but I will be transformed by the renewing of my mind that I may be able to determine your will — your good, pleasing and perfect will for my life. (Romans 12:1, 2)

I ask you to help me be a wise son who brings joy to his Father. (Proverbs 15:20) *Come and build my house through me today that I labor not in vain.* (Psalm 127:1)

Open my ears to hear what your Spirit is saying for ears that hear and eyes that see - the Lord has made them both. (Proverbs 20:12 NIV)

Open my eyes that I may see in wisdom and revelation that I may know you better (Ephesians 1:17); *and that I may see wonderful things in your word.* (Psalm 119:18)

Set a guard over my mouth, keep watch over the door of my lips (Psalm 141:3). *May the words of my mouth and the meditation of my heart be pleasing in your sight, my Rock and my Redeemer.* (Psalm 19:14)

Let my mouth be a fountain of life (Proverbs 10:11), *may my lips nourish many* (Proverbs 10:21), *and my tongue be as choice silver.* (Proverbs 10:20)

Train my hands for war and my fingers for battle (Psalm 144:1); *whatever my hands find to do, help me to do it with all my might.* (Ecclesiastes 9:10)

Direct my steps according to your word. (Psalm 119:133) *Teach me to number my days aright that I may gain a heart of wisdom.* (Psalm 90:12)

In Jesus' Name, Amen."

How to Pray for Your Husband

Although I mentioned this before, let me state this again for emphasis. As a wife, you know and love your husband better than anyone else; therefore, the Lord will show you the weak areas in his life that He will not entrust to others. He does not do this for you to point out publicly, expose to your friends and relatives, or nag him daily to correct him. No, the Lord wants you to pray for him. He will give you a specific scripture to counteract this weak point so that your husband may grow strong in the Lord through your life-giving prayers.

I would like to encourage the wives to pray, "Open my eyes that I may see wonderful things in your law" (Psalm 119:18) concerning your husband. The Holy Spirit will begin to enlighten certain verses for you to pray over him as a means of building him up in the Spirit.

One of my husband's favorite quotes of the late missionary evangelist, T. L. Osbourne, has become a guiding principle in our lives: "Always esteem, never demean." This is based on the scriptures of Ephesians 4:29-32.*

There was a time when I kept hearing "boldness" for my husband. I began to pray Proverbs 28:1, "the righteous are bold as a lion;" Psalm 138:3, "when I called, you answered me and made me bold and stouthearted"; and II Timothy 1:7 (NIV), "for you have not given me the spirit of timidity but of power, love and self-discipline." Within three weeks, my husband was walking with a new mantel of strength, power and boldness.

About this same time, I began to hear "discernment" every time I prayed for John. The Lord gave me many scriptures in the Proverbs to pray: Proverbs 18:15, "The heart of the discerning acquires knowledge"; Proverbs 14:6 [b], "Knowledge comes easily to the discerning"; Proverbs 14:33, "Wisdom reposes in the heart of the discerning." Also, Psalm 119:125, Proverbs 15:14, Proverbs 16:21.

I thought he just needed discernment to direct the prayer ministry at our church. However, a year and a half later we received a word from the Lord that the cloak of discernment was falling upon him to discern the principalities controlling the different cities across the United States in order that we can pull down the strongholds that hold the cities captive.

We only see life through our limited, finite perception, but when we allow the Holy Spirit to direct our prayers, He begins to pour out His heart to us and make His thoughts known to us. (Proverbs 1:23 NIV)

In addition to seeing your husband become all he is supposed to be in God, you will reap into your own life all the gifts, power and anointing the Lord pours into him because you are one in the Spirit.

Pray: "THY KINGDOM COME, THY WILL BE DONE IN MY HUSBAND'S LIFE AS IT IS IN HEAVEN.

Father, blessed is my husband, _____, who does not walk in the counsel of the wicked, or stand in the way of sinners or sit in the seat of mockers. But his delight is in the law of the Lord and on his law, he meditates day and night. He is like a tree planted by streams of water, which yields its fruit in season and whose leaf does not wither. Whatever he does prospers. (Psalm 1:1-3 NIV)

The Spirit of the Lord will rest upon my husband, the Spirit of wisdom and of understanding —the Spirit of counsel and of power, the Spirit of knowledge and of the fear of the Lord —and he will delight in the fear of the Lord. (Isaiah 11:2, 3 NIV)

May the favor of the Lord our God rest upon my husband; establish the work of his hands for him – yes, establish the work of his hands. (Psalm 90:17)

The Lord will fulfill his purpose in my husband's life; your love, O Lord, endures forever - do not abandon the works of your hands. (Psalm 138:8)

I pray that my husband may prosper in all things and be in health just as his soul prospers. (III John 1:2)

Open my husband's eyes that he may see wonderful things in your law. (Psalm 119:18)

Your hands made him and formed him; give him understanding to learn your commands. (Psalm 119:73)

The King's heart is in the hand of the Lord; he directs it like a watercourse wherever he pleases. (Proverbs 21:1)

Blessed is my husband who fears the Lord, who finds great delight in his commands. His children will be mighty in the land; each generation of the upright will be blessed. Wealth and riches are in his house, and his righteousness endures forever. Even in darkness light dawns for the upright, for the gracious and compassionate and righteous man. Good will come to him who is generous and lends freely, who conducts his affairs with justice. Surely, he will never be shaken; a righteous man will be remembered forever. He will have no fear of bad news; his heart is steadfast, trusting in the Lord. His heart is secure, he will have no fear; in the end he will look in triumph on his foes. He has scattered abroad his gifts to the poor, his righteousness endures forever; his horn (dignity) will be lifted high in honor. The wicked man will see and be vexed, he will gnash his teeth and waste away; the longings of the wicked will come to nothing. (Psalm 112)

No eye has seen, no ear has heard, no mind has conceived what God has prepared for those who love him, but God has revealed it to us by his Spirit. The Spirit searches all things, even the deep things of God. (I Corinthians 2:9) *[It will be better than all your planning — Mrs. James Watt.]*

I keep asking that the God of our Lord Jesus Christ, the glorious Father, may give my husband the Spirit of wisdom and revelation, so that he may know Him better. (Ephesians 1:17)

To the man who pleases him, God gives wisdom, knowledge, and happiness, and to the sinner he gives the task of gathering and storing up wealth to hand over to the one who pleases God. (Ecclesiastes 2:26)

You will instruct my husband and teach him in the way he should go; you will counsel him and watch over him...but the Lord's unfailing love surrounds the man who trusts in him. (Psalm 32:8, 10 NIV)

For the Lord gives wisdom, and from his mouth come knowledge and understanding. "(Proverbs 2:6 NIV)

"Do not let any unwholesome talk come out of your mouths, but only what is helpful for building others up according to

their needs, that it may benefit those who listen. And do not grieve the Holy Spirit of God…Get rid of all bitterness, rage and anger, brawling and slander, along with every form of malice. Be kind and compassionate to one another, forgiving each other, just as in Christ God forgave you." (Ephesians 4:29-32 NIV) *

In Jesus' Name, Amen."

How to Pray for Your Wife

I would like to encourage the husbands with the words of Paul:

"Husbands, love your wives and do not be harsh with them." (Colossians 3:19 NIV)

"For the husband is the head of the wife as Christ is the head of the church, his body, of which he is the Savior. Now as the church submits to Christ, so also wives should submit to their husbands in everything. Husbands, *love your wives, just as Christ loved the church* and gave himself up for her." (Ephesians 5:23-25 NIV) [Emphasis mine]

The same principles apply for husbands to pray for their wives. Pray specific scriptures over the weak areas of your wife's life in order to build her up spiritually. ("Always esteem, never demean." T. L. Osbourne)

Harsh words and scolding will not knit you together but rather drive you further apart. A Pastor friend of ours always taught that the "Kindest word is an unkind word never spoken." You can choose to live in peace with your wife or ...always be right. However, when you allow the Holy Spirit to use you as her spiritual authority, she will respond to your gentle, loving corrections and insight.

As you strengthen your wife daily in the place of prayer, she will not only blossom into the wife of noble character found in Proverbs 31, but your marriage will become *"a chord of three strands...not quickly broken"*. (Ecclesiastes 4:12 NIV) She will walk by your side spiritually and help you become a man who *"is respected at the city gate, where he takes his seat among the elders of the land."* (Proverbs 31:23 NIV) Together you will fulfill His purpose in your lives and accomplish great and mighty things for the Kingdom of God. (I have heard my husband pray these scriptures over me many many times).

"THY KINGDOM COME, THY WILL BE DONE IN MY WIFE'S LIFE AS IT IS IN HEAVEN!

Father, my wife, _____, is a wise woman who builds her house, but with her own hands the foolish one tears hers down. (Proverbs 14:1 NIV)

Unless the Lord builds the house, she labors in vain. Unless the Lord watches over the city, the watchmen stand guard in vain. (Psalm 127:1 NIV)

A wife of noble character who can find? I thank you, Lord that my wife will be of noble character today. She is worth far more than rubies. I, her husband, have full confidence in her and will lack nothing of value. She will bring me good, not harm, all the days of her life. She selects wool and flax and works with eager hands. She is like the merchant ships, bringing her food from afar. She gets up while it is still dark; she provides food for her family and portions for her servant girls. She considers a field and buys it; out of her earnings, she plants a vineyard. She sets about her work vigorously; help her arms to be strong for her tasks today. Help her to see that her trading is profitable, and her lamp will not go out at night. In her hand, she holds the distaff and grasps the spindle with her fingers. (Help her to be industrious today, establish the work of her hands for her [Psalm 90:17]). She opens her arms to the poor and extends her hands to the needy. When it snows, she has no fear for her household; for all of them are clothed in scarlet. She makes coverings for her bed; she is clothed in fine linen and purple. Her husband will be respected at the city gate (in the community) where I will take my seat among the elders of the land. She makes linen garments and sells them, and supplies the merchants with sashes. She is clothed in strength and dignity; she can laugh at the days to come. She speaks with wisdom, and faithful instruction is on her tongue. She watches over the affairs of her household and does not eat the bread of idleness. Her children arise and call her blessed; I, her husband, will praise her; many women do noble things, but she surpasses them all. Charm is deceptive, and beauty is fleeting; but a woman who fears the Lord is to be praised. Give her the reward she has earned, and let her works bring her praise at the city gate. (Proverbs 31:10-31 NIV) *[Emphasis mine]*

Though one may be overpowered, two can defend themselves. Knit our hearts together, O Lord, to stand against the schemes of the enemy that assault our marriage, for a cord of three strands is not quickly broken. (Ecclesiastes 4:12)

My wife's heart will not envy sinners but will always be zealous for the fear of the Lord. There is surely a future hope for her, and her hope will not be cut off. (Proverbs 23:17-18)

The Lord is my wife's light and her salvation – whom shall she fear? The Lord is the stronghold of her life – of whom shall she be afraid? When evil men advance against her to devour her flesh, when her enemies and her foes attack her, they will stumble and fall. Though an army besiege her, her heart will not fear; though war break out against her, even then will she be confident. (Psalm 27:1-3)

How to Pray for Your Children

Parents do not exasperate your children; instead, bring them up in the training and instruction of the Lord.
(Ephesians 6:4 NIV)

If there is anything, I can say to the parents, it is to *"guard your heart for it is the wellspring of life."* (PROVERBS 4:23 NIV) Remember, your children have been placed in your home only for a season.

You have been given a precious gift to have the opportunity to be a parent entrusted with God's precious treasures. He wants to use your home as a training ground for the next generation's John Wesleys, Billy Grahams, Kathryn Kulhmans, pastors evangelists, or missionaries, as well as, leaders in government and business... He wants our children to rise up and *"be mighty in the land"* (Psalm 112:1 NIV) in whatever walk of life they fulfill.

Remember, our children are on a journey in life that we will not complete with them. They will continue to travel without us and only take with them what we have taught them. This sobering thought emphasizes the importance of the scripture found in Proverbs 22:6, " Train up a child in the way he should go and when he is old, he will not depart from it." KJV

I continually ask the Lord to show my little girls to me through His eyes and sensitize my ears to the cry of their hearts. Behind their words, I want to "hear" what they are trying to say to me and be able to discern rightly.

"THY KINGDOM COME, THY WILL BE DONE IN MY CHILDREN'S LIVES AS IT IS IN HEAVEN!

Father, your Word says to train a child in the way he should go and when he is old, he will not depart from it. Help me, Lord, to train my children today in the way you would have them to go. (Proverbs 22:6)

All my sons will be taught by the Lord and great will be my children's peace. Teach through me today, Father, and let my children hear your voice within my voice and the voice of their teachers this day. (Isaiah 54:13)

May they apply their hearts to instruction and their ears to words of knowledge. (Proverbs 23:12)

44

For the Lord gives wisdom, and from his mouth come knowledge and understanding. (Proverbs 2:6) *Father, grant my children wisdom today, and may they receive knowledge and understanding from your Word.*

Ears that hear and eyes that see, the Lord has made them both (Proverbs 20:12). *Give my children ears that will hear the voice of your Holy Spirit today, and let them see not as the world sees, but by your Spirit in wisdom and revelation.*

Turn the hearts of the fathers to their children and the hearts of the children to their fathers (Malachi 4:6). *May my children always love and respect not only their natural father, but their heavenly Father as well, and may my husband always remain tender and sensitive to the jewels the Lord has placed in our care for a season.*

And just as Jesus grew in wisdom and stature and in favor with God and men, let it be so for my children. (Luke 2:52)

Father, your Word says a wise son brings joy to his father (Proverbs 10:1 [a]). *Let my children be wise and bring their father joy this day.*

Father, let my children pay attention to what I say and listen closely to my words. Do not let them out of their sight, help them keep them within their hearts; for they are life to those who find them and health to a man's whole body. Above all else, help them to guard their heart, (build a hedge of protection about them), for it is the wellspring of life. (Proverbs 4:20-23)

My children obey their parents in everything, for this pleases the Lord. Their father does not embitter his children, or they will become discouraged. (Colossians 3:20-21)

Father, your Word says, Believe in the Lord Jesus, and you will be saved — you and your household. (Acts 16:31)

Do not withhold discipline from a child; if you punish him with the rod, he will not die. Punish him with the rod and save his soul from death. (Proverbs 23:13-14)

Show me your ways, O Lord, teach me your paths; guide me in your truth and teach me, for you are God my Savior, and my hope is in you all day long. Remember, O Lord, your great mercy and love, for they are from of old. Remember not the sins of my youth and my rebellious ways; according to your love remember me, for you are good, O Lord. (Psalm 25:4-7) *Show my children your ways, Lord.*

Praise be to the Lord, for He has heard my cry for mercy. The Lord is my strength and my shield; my heart trusts in Him, and I am helped. (Psalm 28:6-7)

The righteous man leads a blameless life, blessed are his children after him. (Proverbs 20:7)

Even a child is known by his actions, by whether his conduct is pure and right. (Proverbs 20:11)

Folly is bound up in the heart of a child, but the rod of discipline will drive it far from him. (Proverbs 22:15)

Children's children are a crown to the aged, and parents are the pride of their children. (Proverbs 17:6)

Father, I will discipline my son (children) in that there is hope; I will not be a willing party to his (their) death. (Proverbs 19:18)

In Jesus' Name, Amen."

The Lord's Prayer for Children

When the Lord first asked me what kind of house I would build for Him, I did not know what He meant, but I told him, "Any kind you want." As I began to pray for my family that morning, He said to me, "When **you** become a house of prayer, your **family** will be a house of prayer, and your **ministry** will be a house of prayer."

Do you see the progression? I had to become a house of prayer before my family would be a house of prayer, and our family had to become a house of prayer before our ministry would be a house of prayer.

After I learned to pray faithfully over my children, the Lord began to impress me that it was time for them to learn to pray effectively and defeat the enemy in their lives. At this point, we were still struggling with fearfulness and sickness in our children. The Lord told me to saturate their spirits with the Word for:

"The entrance of your words gives light; it gives understanding to the simple." (Psalm 119:130 NIV)

"For the Lord gives wisdom, and from his mouth come knowledge and understanding." (Proverbs 2:6 NIV)

"All your sons will be taught by the Lord and great will be your children's peace." (Isaiah 54:13 NIV)

The Lord was teaching me how to use "the word which is the sword of the Spirit" to break the chains that were binding my children.

Every school year presented a different set of challenges with friendships, teachers, academic subjects and school activities. The scripture in Psalm 119:130 was made real to us in many ways, *the entrance of the word brings light, it gives understanding to the simple.* We found the more of the Word of God we memorized and prayed daily, the more understanding our children had in school and the more understanding we had in our challenges at work or in ministry. Then entrance of the Word, God's Words, God's thoughts...instructs us and opens our understanding with His wisdom and insight.

One young mother I prayed with in the early morning prayer meetings, related to me that her little boy could not read until she had him memorize scriptures. His little mind then opened and he became one of the top students in his class! The Word works!

We prayed on the way to school in the mornings to sensitize the spirits of our children to the Holy Spirit for instruction throughout the day. (It was also a good way to keep them from fighting!) It took one school year or approximately eight months for our four year old and our nine year old to learn the following outline of the Lord's Prayer based on Dr. Larry Lea's *Could you Not Tarry One Hour?* teaching. We memorized one scripture each week. This is only a beginning point for your children that will take about five minutes to pray through to completion and will help you disciple your children in prayer. It is a *foundation*, however, that they can *build* upon it the rest of their lives!

THE LORD'S PRAYER

"OUR FATHER WHICH ART IN HEAVEN, HALLOWED BE THY NAME,

A. *I will praise thee; for I am fearfully and wonderfully made.* (Psalm 139:14 [a])

B. Thank you for the blood of Jesus and for being:

1. Jehovah-Tsidkenu, my righteousness;

   The righteous are bold as a lion, the wicked man flees with no one pursuing him. (Proverbs 28:1)

2. Jehovah-M'Kaddesh, my sanctification;

Create in me a clean heart, O God; and renew a right spirit within me. (Psalm 51:10)

3. Jehovah-Shalom, my peace;

    I will Trust in the Lord with all mine heart; and lean not unto mine own understanding. In all my ways acknowledge Him, and He shall direct my paths. (Proverbs 3:5, 6)

    I choose to Seek first the Kingdom of God, and his righteousness; and all these things shall be added unto me. (Matthew 6:33)

    For all things work together for good to them that love God, to them who are the called according to His purpose. (Romans 8:28)

4. Jehovah-Shammah, ever present with me;

    You said to Call to me and I will answer you and tell you great and unsearchable things you do not know. (Jeremiah 33:3)

5. Jehovah-Rophe, my healer;

    ...by his stripes we are healed. (Isaiah 53:5 [d])

6. Jehovah-Jirah, my provider;

    ...according to His riches in glory. (Philippians 4:19)

7. Jehovah-Nissi, our protector;

...his banner over us is love. (Song OF SOLOMON 2:4 [b])

His hedge of protection is around us (Job 1:10); and

...his favor guards us as a shield. (Psalm 5:12 [b]).

8. Jehovah-Rohi, the kind and gentle shepherd;

He leads us beside the still waters and makes us lie down in green pastures. (Psalm 23:2)

THY KINGDOM COME, THY WILL BE DONE in my life as it is in heaven:

A. Open my ears to hear what the Spirit is saying. (Proverbs 23:12)

Open my eyes to see in wisdom and revelation. (Ephesians 1:17)

Set a guard over my mouth and keep watch over the door of my lips. (Psalm 141:3 NIV)

May the words of my mouth and the meditation of my heart be pleasing in your sight, O Lord, my Rock and my Redeemer. (Psalm 19:14 NIV)

A soft answer turns away wrath, but a harsh word stirs up anger. (Proverbs 15:1)

Train my hands for war and my fingers for battle. (Psalm 144:1)

Whatever my hands find to do, help me to do it with all my might. (Ecclesiastes 9:10)

Direct my steps according to your Word. (Proverbs 16:9)

Teach me to number my days aright that I may gain a heart of wisdom. (Psalm 90:12 NIV)

B. Fill us with the fruit of the Spirit,

which is love, joy, peace, patience, kindness, goodness, faithfulness, gentleness and self-control. (Galatians 5:22 NIV)

C. In the Name of Jesus and in the power of His blood, we bind the hindering spirits off our lives of frustration, confusion and distraction, and we loose the Spirit of the Lord:

the Spirit of wisdom and understanding, knowledge and discernment and discipline. (Isaiah 11:2, Proverbs 14:6, Proverbs 6:23)

D. In the Name of Jesus and in the power of His blood, we bind the hindering spirits of selfishness, jealousy, envy, fighting and anger, and we loose the spirit of love;

for Love is patient, love is kind. It does not envy, it does not boast, it is not proud or rude or self-seeking, it is not easily angered or keep any record of wrongs. It does not delight in evil but rejoices in the truth. It always protects, always

54

trusts, always hopes, always perseveres. (I Corinthians 13:4-7 NIV)

E. May the favor of the Lord our God rest upon us and may He establish the work of our hands for us. (Proverbs 90:17 NIV)

And for Mommy and Daddy, our Pastor(s) _____ our teacher(s), _____ and our President,

"Remove the wicked from the king's presence, and his throne will be established in righteousness." (Proverbs 25:5)

"Then the righteous will gather around him because of your goodness to him." (Psalm 142:7)

F. *Fulfill your purpose in us, O Lord, for your love endures forever - do not abandon the work of your hands.* (Proverbs 138:8 NIV)

GIVE US THIS DAY OUR DAILY BREAD:

We stand in agreement together for all our needs to be met:

a. _____

_____

b. _____

_____

c. _____

_____

FORGIVE US OUR DEBTS AS WE FORGIVE OUR DEBTORS:

We choose to walk in love and forgiveness. Forgive me, Father, when I have offended you: _____ (name specific offense).

AND LEAD US NOT INTO TEMPTATION, BUT DELIVER US FROM EVIL:

A. *Put on the whole armor of God, that ye may be able to stand against the wiles of the devil.* (Ephesians 6:11)

B. *We gird our loins about with truth, we put on the breastplate of righteousness. We shod our feet with the readiness of the gospel of peace and pull down the helmet of salvation. We take out our sword of the spirit and shield of faith.* (Ephesians 6:14-17)

C. The hedge of protection is around us;

D. *The angel of the Lord encamps around those who fear Him, and He delivers them.* (Psalm 34:7 NIV)

FOR THINE IS THE KINGDOM AND THE POWER AND THE GLORY FOREVER! AMEN."

(Sing a chorus of praise together!)

How to Pray for Your Parents

"Children obey your parents in the Lord, for this is right.
'Honor your father and mother' - which is the first
commandment with a promise - 'that it may go well with
you and that you may enjoy long life on the earth.'"
(Ehpesians 6:1-3 NIV)

It is our Father's desire that we love and honor our parents. In fact, as noted in the above scripture and Deuteronomy 5:16 it is the first *commandment* with a promise: *"it will go well with you and that you may enjoy long life on the earth."* [Emphasis mine]

It will go well with us (the favor and blessings of God will be ours) that we may enjoy a long life - how beautiful! Not a life filled with trouble and heartache, but a long life full of blessings, honor, and favor.

Some of us had loving, caring, nurturing parents who did their very best to provide, teach, train us in godly ways. Others sadly, did not. I will address this as well in a moment.

Unfortunately, ALL parents make mistakes and need to be forgiven..."All have sinned and fall short..."

- In homes of the God loving, caring, and nurturing- parents fall short.

- In homes of dysfunctional alcoholic or drug addicts- parents fall short.

- In homes of working or business minded parents - parents fall short.

Unfortunately, no matter what the circumstance, all parents fall short at some level.

The command is still there to "honor your parents". It is not a suggestion or qualified by certain circumstances:

"If" you have a good relationship;

"If" they did nearly everything right;

"if" they were present and not absent;

"If" they were good providers

"if" _____

(You fill in the blank of hurts, or disappointments).

Let's address the dysfunctional homes. Your parents may have been abusive, anything but nurturing, and life at home was simply a place to escape as soon as possible. I have a special admonition for you, as well as the rest of us, which is not easy, but it is the only way: Forgive.

We must all forgive our parents. The hurtful chains of the past will be broken and we will be able to walk into freedom for our futures. Freedom from the hurt, pain and wounds of childhood. Free to be the person God wants us to be - a better stronger person instead of a bitter person chained to the past.

These scriptures will heal our hearts as we declare, "Father, I choose to forgive my parents. I choose to forgive the hurtful words, the fighting, anger, strife and abuse. I choose to forgive the unjustness. I choose to forgive their faults and failures. Your Word is true:

"Love covers a multitude of sins." Proverbs 10:12

"Our faith works by love." Galatians 5:36

"Love never fails." I Corinthians 13:8

Father, I now ask you to love my parents through me.

Now let us pray for our parents and remember: "You love who you pray for, who you pray with, and who you pray to." (Ed Cole)

Let us never be found among the Pharisees and teachers of the law rebuked by Jesus in Mark 7:11 for refusing to help their fathers and mothers:

"But you say that if a man says to his father or mother: 'Whatever help you might otherwise have received from me is Corban' (that is, a gift devoted to God), then you no longer let him do anything for his father or mother. Thus you nullify the word of God..."

Let it be said of us instead that we are wise sons that bring joy to our father's heart (Proverbs 15:20).

"THY KINGDOM COME THY WILL BE DONE IN MY PARENTS LIVES AS IT IS IN HEAVEN.

Father, I thank you for my parents and for the love we share. Help me to honor them all the days of their lives that it will go well with my household and that we may enjoy long life on this earth.

I pray that the latter part of their lives will be more blessed than the beginning (Job 42:12).

I thank you that because of their faithfulness they will be richly blessed (Proverbs 28:20); and because they have given to the poor they will lack nothing (Proverbs 28:27).

Keep them from the snares that have been laid for them, from the traps set by evil doers. Let the wicked fall into their own nets, while they pass by in safety (Psalm 141:9, 10).

I pray they will flourish like palm trees and grow like cedars of Lebanon, planted in the house of the Lord. May they still bear fruit in old age, and stay fresh and green, proclaiming: 'The Lord is upright, He is our Rock. (Psalm 92:12-15).

I declare they have been redeemed from the curse of poverty, sickness and disease, and spiritual death (Galatians 3:13, 14). *Not only do they live in abundant prosperity* (Deuteronomy 28:11), *but no sickness and disease shall live in their bodies. In the name of Jesus I curse every infirmity and say you must leave their bodies, you cannot dwell in them. They are a delightful land* (Malachi 3:12). *They will live out all their days strong in the Lord and in the power of His might* (Ephesians 6:10).

I thank you for increasing their wisdom, knowledge and understanding in every area of their lives in order that you may lead and guide them according to your word with no sin ruling over them (Psalm 119:133).

In Jesus' Name, Amen."

(In our fast-paced world filled with work schedules, school activities, and church meetings, not to mention social and community events, the lives of those we love can sometimes slip away from us as they fade into the background of their slower-paced autumn and winter seasons of their lives. Never demanding, but lovingly and supportively, they watch their offspring move into the season of young adulthood tentatively and then more confidently branch out into their specific field to fulfill the call of God on their lives. To these strong, brave men and women, who not only laid their lives down to provide for us, but also had the courage to release their young to the call of life, we must rise to our place of responsibility to uphold their arms in their latter days.)

How to Pray for Your Pastor

There was a time when I prayed for my pastor and church as much or more than my own family. Do not be afraid to flow in the ministry of intercession should the Spirit desire to use you in this manner. You will reap bountifully into your own life as you sow into the life of another.

The following passages will enable you to begin to lift the arms of your pastor even as Aaron and Hur lifted Moses' arms through the long, weary hours of the battle.

"THY KINGDOM COME, THY WILL BE DONE IN MY PASTOR'S LIFE AS IT IS IN HEAVEN!

The Spirit of the Lord will rest upon him - the Spirit of wisdom and of understanding, the Spirit of counsel and of power, the Spirit of knowledge and of the fear of the Lord - and he will delight in the fear of the Lord. (Isaiah 11:2, 3)

No one from the east or the west or from the desert can exalt a man. But it is God who judges; He brings one down, He exalts another. I will cut off the horns of all the wicked, but the horns of the righteous will be lifted up. (Psalm 75:6, 7, 10)

Neither before nor after Josiah was there a king like him who turned to the Lord as he did - with all his heart and with all his soul and with all his strength. (II Kings 23:25) *May the spirit of Josiah rest upon my pastor as he turns to you with all his heart, soul and strength.*

May the favor of the Lord our God rest upon us and may he establish the work of our hands for us. (Psalm 90:17)

The Lord will fulfill His purpose for me (my pastor); your love, O Lord, endures forever - do not abandon the works of your hands. (Psalm 138:8)

May people ever pray for him and bless him all day long. (Psalm 72:15 [b])

I keep asking the God of our Lord Jesus Christ, the glorious Father, may give you the Spirit of wisdom and revelation so that you may know Him better. (Ephesians 1:17 NIV)

A wise man has great power, and a man of knowledge increases strength; for waging war you need guidance, and for victory many advisers. (Proverbs. 24:5 NIV)

In Jesus' Name, Amen."

How to Pray for the Nation

"If you don't pray, who will?" The Lord impressed this responsibility into my spirit many years ago when we lived approximately 25 miles from Washington, D.C. in northern Virginia. Since that time, I have learned how to pray for our nation. The following scriptures will help you pray over the leaders of our land.

"THY KINGDOM COME, THY WILL BE DONE IN OUR NATION AS IT IS IN HEAVEN!

I will give them an undivided heart and put a new spirit in them; I will remove from them their heart of stone and give them a heart of flesh. Then they will follow my decrees and be careful to keep my laws. They will be my people, and I will be their God. (Ezekiel 11:19, 20 NIV)

No one from the east or the west or from the desert can exalt a man. But it is God who judges; He brings one down, He exalts another. I will cut off the horns of all the wicked, but the horns of the righteous will be lifted up. (Psalm 75:6, 7, 10 NIV)

America

The righteous will never be uprooted, but the wicked will not remain in the *America* *land.* (Proverbs 10:30 NIV)

To show partiality in judging is not good: Whoever says to the guilty, "You are innocent" - peoples will curse him and nations denounce him. But it will go well with *America* *those who convict the guilty, and rich blessing will come upon* *America* *them.* (Proverbs 24:23-25 NIV)

(Psalm 101:8 and 55:9 NIV are particularly effective in silencing the accusations of the enemy against the righteous in the press, and in all areas of your own life to silence the accusations of the enemy, lies and confusion).

America
Every morning I will put to silence the wicked in the land; I *America* *will cut off every evildoer from the city of the Lord.* (Psalm 101:8 NIV)

Confuse the wicked, O Lord, confound their speech, for I see *America* *violence and strife in the city.* (Psalm 55:9 NIV)

For lack of guidance a nation falls, but many advisers make victory sure. (Proverbs 11:14 NIV)
America
Righteousness exalts a nation, but sin is a disgrace to any people. (Proverbs 14:34 NIV)

America who dwells in the shelter of the Most High will rest in the shadow of the Almighty. America will say of the Lord, "He is my refuge and my fortress, my God, in whom I trust." Surely, he will save America from the fowler's snare and from the deadly pestilence. He will cover America with his feathers, and under his wings America will find refuge; his faithfulness will be her shield and rampart. She will not fear the terror of night, nor the arrow that flies by day, nor the pestilence that stalks in the darkness, nor the plague that destroys at midday. A thousand may fall at America's side, ten thousand at her right hand, but it will not come near her. She will only observe with her eyes and see the punishment of the wicked. If America makes the Most High her dwelling - even the Lord, who is our refuge - then no harm will befall her, no disaster will come near her tent. For He will command his angels concerning America to guard her in all her ways; they will lift her up in her hands, so that she will not strike her foot against a stone. She will tread upon the lion and the cobra; she will trample the great lion and the serpent. "Because America loves me," says the Lord, "I will rescue her; I will protect her, for she acknowledges my name. She will call upon me, and I will answer her; I will be with her in trouble, I will deliver her and honor her. With long life will I satisfy her and show her my salvation." (Psalm 91 NIV)

The Lord foils the plans of the nations; he thwarts the purposes of the peoples. But the plans of the Lord stand firm forever, the purposes of his heart through all generations. Blessed is the nation whose God is the Lord, the people he chose for his inheritance. (Psalm 33:10-12 NIV)

In Jesus' Name, Amen."

How to Pray for Lost Loved Ones

This section has been included for lost loved ones and spouses who do not know the Lord or for those whose affections are not what they should be toward the husband or wife.

"THY KINGDOM COME, THY WILL BE DONE IN (your loved one's name) LIFE AS IT IS IN HEAVEN.

Father, you said, "Believe in the Lord Jesus, and you will be saved —you and your household." (Acts 16:31)

In the name of Jesus and through the power of the blood, I come against the powers of darkness that blind their eyes, stop their ears, and block their understanding (Isaiah 6:9, 10); I put you wicked spirits to silence this day (Psalm 101:8); I confuse you, confound your speech (Psalm 55:9), and disperse you from them. I ask you, Father, to send your mighty angels to war in the heavenlies in their behalf (Daniel 10)

...you his angels, you mighty ones who do his bidding, who obey his word. (Psalm 103:20 NIV)

I demolish the arguments and pretentions in their minds that have set themselves up against the knowledge of God and every stronghold in their lives. I ask you, Holy Spirit, to take captive their very thoughts unto the obedience of Christ and draw them to Jesus - to salvation. (II Corinthians 10:3-5)

Wives Praying for Husbands

You are not wrestling against flesh and blood, but against the spiritual forces of evil in the heavenly realms (Ephesians 6:12). Pray II Corinthians 10:3-5 over your husband daily. Demolish the arguments and pretentions in his mind that have set themselves up against the knowledge of God and take captive his very thoughts unto the obedience of Christ.

Ask the Lord to fill his heart with love for you for Ephesians 5:25 **commands**: *"Husbands, love your wives."* Declare Proverbs 5:15-19 to be the picture of your marriage – that your husband will rejoice with the wife of his youth, captivated (intoxicated) by your love. You must win this battle in the spirit realm in order to see results in the physical realm.

"Every morning I will put to silence all the wicked in the land; I will cut off every evildoer from the city of the Lord." (Psalm 101:8) (*Put to silence the demonic voices that are deceiving him within his thoughts.*)

"No weapon that is formed against thee *(your marriage)* shall prosper; and every tongue that shall rise against thee in judgment thou shalt condemn." (Isaiah 54:17)

"Submit yourselves, then, to God. Resist the devil and he will flee from you." (James 4:7 NIV)

Husbands Praying for Wives

You are not wrestling against flesh and blood, but against the spiritual forces of evil in the heavenly realms (Ephesians 6:12). Pray II Corinthians 10:3-5 over your loved one daily. Demolish the arguments and pretentions in her mind that have set themselves up against the knowledge of God and take captive her very thoughts unto the obedience of Christ. In the name of Jesus and in the power of the blood of the Lamb, command the evil forces that are speaking to her mind to be silent:

"Every morning I will put to silence the wicked in the land; I will cut off every evildoer from the city of the Lord." (Psalm 101.8 NIV)

Begin to pray Proverbs 31:10-31 over your wife daily: that she will bring you good and not harm all the days of her life; that she will speak with wisdom, and faithful instruction will be upon her tongue. Declare that she will be *a wise woman* who builds her house (Proverbs 14:1) and that *the Lord will build the house through her* (Psalm 127:1). You must win this battle in the spirit realm to see results in the physical realm.

"No weapon that is formed against thee *(your marriage)* shall prosper; and every tongue that shall rise against thee in judgment thou shalt condemn." (Isaiah 54:17)

"Submit yourselves, then, to God. Resist the devil and he will flee from you." (James 4:7)

How to Pray for Healing

"And if the Spirit of Him who raised Jesus from the dead is living in you, he who raised Christ from the dead will also give life to your mortal bodies through his Spirit, who lives in you." (Romans 8:11 NIV)

"In the Name of Jesus and through the power of His blood, I bind every demonic power that would try to inflict sickness and disease upon (name), and I cast you away from (him/her). You have no authority in (his/her) life and you must go according to the promise in James 4:7:

Submit yourselves, then, to God. Resist the devil, and he will flee from you.

I declare that No weapon formed against _____ shall prosper and every tongue that shall rise against _____
in judgment you shall condemn.
shall be condemned. (Isaiah 54:17)

I speak to every cell in this body and I command you to function as God intended you to function. I command you to line up with the Word of God. I beak every curse off _____ and I declare that you are covered with the blood of the Lamb.

He sent his word and healed them and delivered them from their destruction. (Psalm 107:20 Amp) In the name of Jesus, I send the Word into my body (area of sickness - heart, lungs, back, etc.) and declare I am delivered from all destruction.

I claim the promises in Jeremiah 33:6:

I will heal my people and will let them enjoy abundant peace and security.

He forgives all my sins and heals all my diseases. (Psalm 103:3 NIV)

*But he was wounded for our transgressions, he was bruised for our iniquities; the chastisement of our peace was upon him; and **with his stripes we are healed.** (Isaiah 53:5)* [Emphasis mine]

In Jesus' Name, Amen."

In Yeshua's Name Amen.

How to Pray for Mental Problems

"Every morning I will put to silence the wicked in the land; I will cut off every evildoer from the city of the Lord." (Psalm 101:8 NIV)

"I take authority over every wicked voice that would try to speak into the mind of _____, and I silence you this day. I confuse you and confound your speech (Psalm 55:9 NIV). I disperse you, in Yeshua's *Jesus' name, and declare that _____ is covered with the blood of the Lamb. You will not be able to oppress _____ any longer.*

Now I ask the Holy Spirit to begin to speak to the mind of _____, and I ask the peace of God to flood their very being.

I break every spirit of confusion, distraction, and frustration and I loose the Spirit of the Lord, the spirit of wisdom and understanding, the spirit of counsel and of power, and the spirit of knowledge and the fear of the Lord. (Isaiah 11:2 NIV)

But the Counselor, the Holy Spirit, whom the Father will send in my name, will teach you all things and will remind you of everything I have said to you. Peace I leave with you; my peace I give you. I do not give to you as the world gives. Do not let your hearts be troubled and do not be afraid. (John 14:26, 27 NIV)

I want you to recall the words spoken in the past by the holy prophets and the commands given by our Lord and Savior through your apostles. (II Peter 3:2 NIV)

The Lord is not slow in keeping His promise, as some understand slowness. He is patient with you, not wanting anyone to perish, but everyone to come to repentance. (II Peter 3:9 NIV)

Be still before the Lord and wait patiently for him. (Psalm 37:7 [a] NIV)

I waited patiently for the Lord; he turned to me and heard my cry. *He lifted me out of the slimy pit, out of the mud and mire; he set my feet on a rock and gave me a* **firm place** *to stand. He put a new song in my mouth, a hymn of praise to our God. Many will see and fear and put their trust in the Lord.* **Blessed is the man who makes the Lord his trust.** (Psalm 40:1-4 NIV) *[Emphasis mine]*

Yeshua's
In Jesus' Name, Amen."

How to Pray Over Your Finances

I would like to encourage you to examine your life and make sure you are consistently tithing and sowing your offerings to the Lord. As you begin to declare the following promises over your life, you will realize that the enemy has been trying to steal your inheritance, as a child of Abraham and that you no longer have to live in a state of financial bondage. Follow the principles in His Word and you will "inherit the land" by His Word:

> "Bring ye all the tithes into the storehouse, that there may be meat in mine house, and prove me now herewith," said the Lord of hosts, "if I will not open the windows of heaven, and pour you out a blessing, that there shall not be room enough to receive it. And I will rebuke the devourer for your sakes." (Malachi 3:10, 11)

> "No weapon that is formed against thee shall prosper; and every tongue that shall rise against thee in

judgment thou shalt condemn. This is the heritage of the servants of the Lord, and their righteousness is of me," said the Lord. (Isaiah 54:17)

"Submit yourselves, then, to God. Resist the devil, and he will flee from you. Come near to God and he will come near to you." (James 4:7, 8 NIV)

"I know, Lord, that you walk in the way of righteousness, along the paths of justice, bestowing wealth on those who love you and making their treasuries full (Proverbs 8:20, 21 NIV).

Thank you for your promises: "I would that you prosper and be in health, even as your soul prospers."(III John 1:2.)

I thank you that you have brought us to a place of abundance. (Psalm 66:12 NIV)

I choose to honor the Lord with my wealth, with the first fruits of all my crops (financial endeavors); then my barns will be filled to overflowing and my vats will brim over with new wine. (Proverbs 3:9, 10) *[This is speaking of the promise of plenty; not just barely enough.]*

I thank you that you are sending a blessing on everything I put my hands to and that you will bless me in the land you are giving me. (Deuteronomy 28:8 NIV)

I know that my gifts are credited to my account (Philippians 4:17) *and that they rise as a fragrant offering, an acceptable sacrifice, pleasing to you, my God* (Philippians. 4:18) *who will meet all my needs according to his glorious riches in Christ Jesus.* (Philippians 4:19 NIV)

In Jesus' Name, Amen."

He who gives to the poor will lack nothing (Proverbs 28:27)

Present Your Requests To God

"Do not be anxious about anything, but in everything, by prayer and petition, with thanksgiving, present your requests to God. And the peace of God, which transcends all understanding, will guard your hearts and your minds in Christ Jesus." **(Philippians 4:6, 7 NIV)**

Do not be afraid to bring your needs to the Lord. He is concerned about every aspect of your life - small or large. Be very specific with your requests and then ask the Lord to open your eyes that you may see His blessings when they come into your life. (Jeremiah 17)

When Hagar was cast into the desert with her son, Ishmael, *God* **opened her eyes** *and she* **saw** *a well of water* (Genesis 21:19); which was God's provision. When Abraham went to sacrifice Isaac, the promised son, the Lord provided a substitute: *Abraham looked up* and there in a thicket he saw a ram caught by its horns. (Genesis 22:13 NIV) As the servant prayed concerning a wife for Isaac, the Word says,

before he had finished praying, *Rebekah came out with her jar on her shoulder.* (Genesis 24:15 NIV) *Without saying a word, the man* **watched her closely** *to learn whether the Lord had made his journey successful.* (Genesis 24:21)

{ "Before they call I will answer; while they are still speaking I will hear." (Isaiah 65:24 NIV) }

The Lord is working all things together for good from the first day you begin to pray. Read Daniel chapter 10 about the great war in the heavenlies to detain the answer to his prayers for three weeks. Do not grow discouraged. You will reap if ye faint not, whether it takes a week, a month, or a year for your seeds of prayer to grow into manifestation.

Preferred Reading List

Could You Not Tarry One Hour? Dr. Larry Lea

Why Pray? Dr. B. J. Willhite

How Much Faith Does it Take to Move the Hand of God? Dr. B. J. Willhite

Proof Producers Dr. Morris Cerullo

Fasting Jentezen Franklin

The 21 Day Fast Dr. Bob Rodgers

Faith & Confessions Charles Capps

The Basics of Hospice Chaplain Ministry, Practical Help for the New Chaplain John M. Casto, Board Certified Chaplain